INDIA
AND
SRI LANKA

Cultures and Costumes Series:

CULTURES AND COSTUMES: SYMBOLS OF THEIR PERIOD

INDIA
AND
SRI LANKA

CONOR KILGALLON

Summit Free Public Library

MASON CREST PUBLISHERS

www.masoncrest.com

Mason Crest Publishers, Inc.
370 Reed Road
Broomall, PA 19008
(866) MCP-BOOK (toll free)
www.masoncrest.com

13 12 11 10 09 08 07   10 9 8 7 6 5 4 3 2

Library of Congress Cataloging-in-Publication Data

Kilgallon, Conor.
  India and Sri Lanka / Conor Kilgallon.
      v. cm. — (Cultures and costumes)
Includes bibliographical references and index.
Contents: An ancient land—The golden age and the first Muslims—New
Invaders: the Moguls and the British — Ceremonies, rituals, and festivals —The island of Sri Lanka.
  ISBN 1-59084-443-2 (Hard cover)
1. Clothing and dress—India—History—Juvenile literature.
2. Clothing and dress—Sri Lanka—History—Juvenile literature.
3. India—Social life and customs—Juvenile literature.
4. Sri Lanka—Social life and customs—Juvenile literature.
[1. Clothing and dress—India—History. 2. Clothing and dress—Sri Lanka—
History. 3. India—Social life and customs. 4. Sri Lanka—Social life
and customs] I. Title. II. Series.
  GT1460'.K55 2003
  391'.00954—dc21   2003000892

Printed and bound in Malaysia

Editorial and design by
Amber Books Ltd.
Bradley's Close
74–77 White Lion Street
London N1 9PF

Project Editor: Marie-Claire Muir
Design: Hawes Design
Picture Research: Lisa Wren

Picture Credits:
All pictures courtesy of Amber Books Ltd, except the following:
The National Library of Australia: 50

ACKNOWLEDGMENT
For authenticating this book, the Publishers would like to thank Robert L. Humphrey. Jr., Professor Emeritus of Anthropology, George Washington University, Washington, D.C.

Contents

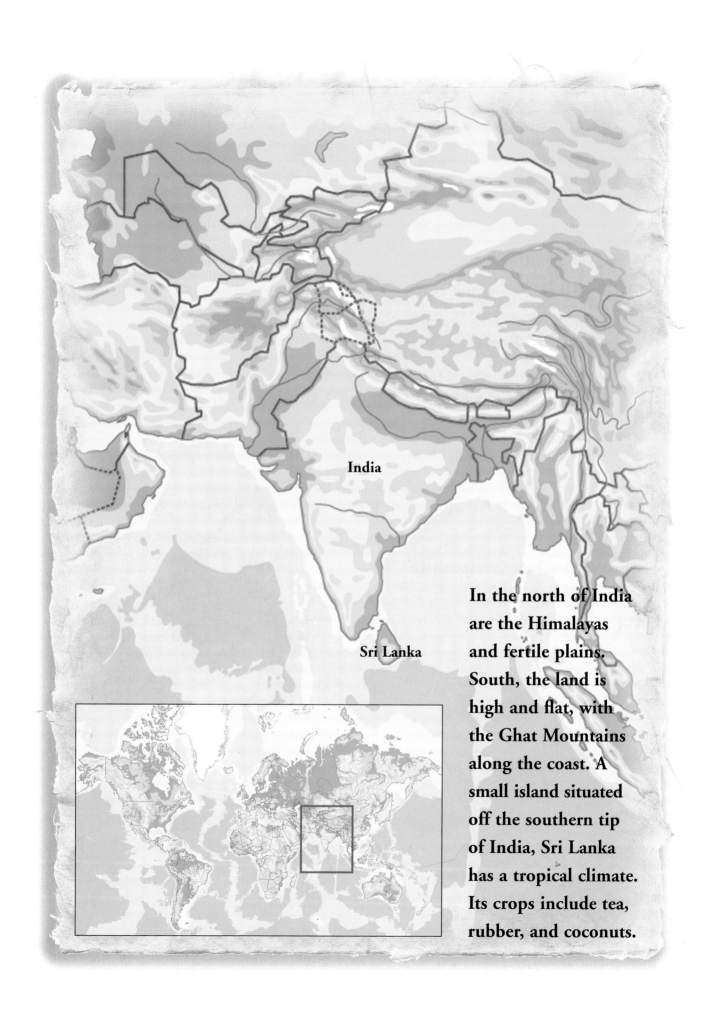

India

Sri Lanka

In the north of India are the Himalayas and fertile plains. South, the land is high and flat, with the Ghat Mountains along the coast. A small island situated off the southern tip of India, Sri Lanka has a tropical climate. Its crops include tea, rubber, and coconuts.

Introduction

Nearly every species in the animal kingdom adapts to changes in the environment. To cope with cold weather, the cat adapts by growing a longer coat of fur, the bear hibernates, and birds migrate to a different climatic zone. Only humans use costume and culture—what they have learned through many generations—to adapt to the environment.

The first humans developed their culture by using spears to hunt the bear, knives and scrapers to skin it, and needles and sinew to turn the hide into a warm coat to insulate their hairless bodies. As time went on, the clothes humans wore became an indicator of cultural and individual differences. Some were clearly developed to be more comfortable in the environment, others were designed for decorative, economic, political, and religious reasons.

Ritual costumes can tell us about the deities, ancestors, and civil and military ranking in a society, while other clothing styles can identify local or national identity. Social class, gender, age, economic status, climate, profession, and political persuasion are also reflected in clothing. Anthropologists have even tied changes in the hemline length of women's dresses to periods of cultural stress or relative calm.

In 13 beautifully illustrated volumes, the *Cultures and Costumes: Symbols of their Period* series explores the remarkable variety of costumes found around the world and through different eras. Each book shows how different societies have clothed themselves, revealing a wealth of diverse and sometimes mystifying explanations. Costume can be used as a social indicator by scientists, artists, cinematographers, historians, and designers—and also provide students with a better understanding of their own and other cultures.

ROBERT L. HUMPHREY, JR., Professor Emeritus of Anthropology,
George Washington University, Washington, D.C.

An Ancient Land

"India is the cradle of the human race, the birthplace of human speech, the mother of history, grandmother of legend, and great-grandmother of tradition. Our most valuable and most instructive materials in the history of man are treasured up in India only."

So wrote the American author Mark Twain (1835–1910) about the great land that lies south of the Himalayas, flanked by the Arabian Sea and the Bay of Bengal. Few countries in the world have a culture and history as old and diverse as India. With its beginnings going back 5,000 years, it was one of the first regions to produce a civilization. Over this time, India's culture has been altered by waves of invaders from other regions, including Europe, the Middle East, and China, whose own cultures were absorbed into the Indian way of life.

The Ancient Cities

Ancient Indian people, known as the Harrapans, were highly advanced. Around 2500 B.C. in northern India, they built cities out of brick, kept domesticated animals, and produced metals such as copper, bronze, lead, and tin.

With these metals, they made necklaces, anklets, rings, earrings, and nose studs. For clothing, vegetable bark, animal skins, and cotton and wool were

These women are Kathak dancers. They are wearing *chuni* scarves, *salwar* trousers, and sheer tunics. On their heads they wear large veils that billow out as they dance.

used. Fabric was highly prized, and the Harrapans knew how to incorporate decorative elements into the weaving process. These fabrics were then either worn unstitched, as a single piece of cloth simply wrapped around the body, or cut up into specific shapes and stitched together to make a fitted garment, such as a coat or trousers. A piece of ancient pottery found by **archaeologists** shows an old man with a cropped beard wearing a headband, an **armlet**, and a shawl with **embroidery** on it around his shoulders.

Between 1800 and 1700 B.C., the Harrapan civilization disappeared. Some think the warlike Aryans, a tribe that invaded northern India, crushed them. Others believe that the nearby river, the Indus, flooded the Harrapan towns.

The Aryan Invaders

The Aryans invaded India from Afghanistan in around 1500 B.C. Calling themselves "the noble ones," they were a tough, warlike people who lived as **nomadic** farmers. The Vedic civilization they started was a new beginning for Indian culture after the disappearance of the Harrapans. In fact, the Aryans adopted almost nothing of Harrapan culture. Instead, they were a warrior people who organized themselves into tribal units, called the *jana,* ruled over by a war chief, or *raja*.

Despite their initial lack of sophistication, the Aryans were crucial to the development of Indian culture. They introduced the horse, developed the ancient Indian language (called Sanskrit), and started the religion that formed the basis of Hinduism, which is now practiced by 80 percent of Indian people.

Socially, the early Aryans had only two classes, the nobles and the commoners. Later, society settled into four rigid classes, or castes, called the *caturvarnas,* or "four colors." At the top were the priests (Brahmans), then came the nobles (Kshatriya), then the craftspeople and merchants (Vaishya), and last, at the bottom, were the servants (Shudra). These class boundaries were completely inflexible and were strongly linked to the religion of the time. The caste system still exists in India today, and is the subject of much controversy.

The ox and cart has been a form of transport in India since ancient times. This man is a local official, as can be seen from the designs on the side of the cart, the presence of a driver, and the oxen draped in fabric.

It was during this time that many textiles and designs were invented and named. Paintings from Vedic times are scarce (the Aryans were not interested in art), but their writings are full of names and descriptions of fabrics and clothes. In these ancient times, and for several centuries afterward, Indian women either left their upper body naked or supported their breasts with a strip of fabric knotted at the front (this was not really intended to provide any covering). The majority of women dressed in unstitched lengths of cotton fabric. Regional styles, still common today in India, were created by draping, knotting, and combining the fabrics in different ways.

The nobility dressed in a similar manner, but the quality of their cloth was far higher. Finest-quality wools, cottons, and imported silks were used. A desire

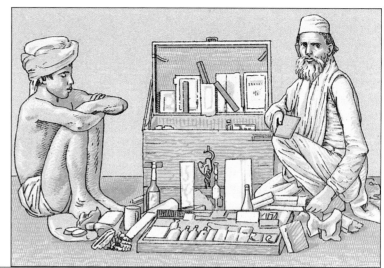

The medicine man, the trader using his weighing scales, and the carpenter are all Indian professionals wearing stitched upper garments and unstitched lower ones.

to own the finest garments, made of the finest fabrics, has been a hallmark of Indian costume ever since. Dress consisted of the *uttariya*, a length of cloth draped across the upper part of the body, the *antariya*, a length of cloth wrapped around the lower body, and the *kayabandhan*, a decorative sash tied around the waist to keep the *antariya* in place. These items are still recognizable today in modern Indian costume.

The New Religions

With society divided on the basis of rigid castes, conflicts and upsets were inevitable. In fact, the sixth century B.C. was a time of social and intellectual

The Hindu Gods

Unlike the faithful of other major religions, such as Judaism, Christianity, and Islam, Hindus do not worship only one god. In fact, there is a vast number of gods, and each god has its own personality. However, these gods are arranged into a hierarchy, at the top of which are Brahma, the creator, Vishnu, the preserver, and Shiva, the destroyer of evil.

Along with their own personalities, the gods have their own clothing and associations with clothing. Brahma, for example, is said to have created wool. Shiva has matted hair, in which is said to live Ganga, goddess of the holy Ganges River. Shiva also wears a coiled cobra around his neck and carries a three-pronged spear called a trident.

All Hindu gods—many of which have the head of an animal and six arms—are depicted wearing garlands of flowers around their necks, as well as a lot of jewelry, such as gold and pearl necklaces, along with many bangles on their arms and rings on their fingers and toes. They also wear elaborate crowns made of gold and studded with gems. The gods and goddesses usually wear traditional Indian clothes. Male gods are often naked from the waist up and wear a brightly colored *dhoti* as a lower garment, while female gods wear either a *dhoti*, with a blouse as an upper garment, or a *sari*.

Among the many hundreds of gods is Vishvakarma, the god of craft, who is worshiped by artisans, including textile workers, all around India. His feast day is celebrated every August, and craftsmen lay their tools at the feet of an image of the god and pray for his blessings.

upheaval in India. It was then that Vardhamana Mahavira (ca. 540–468 B.C.) founded the Jain religion, and Siddhartha Gautama (ca. 563–483 B.C.) attained enlightenment, was called Buddha, and formed a new religion, Buddhism. These two religions preached nonviolence to all living creatures, tolerance, and self-discipline. Their teachings were popular due to their simplicity and practicality. Later, Buddhist monks spread their religion to Sri Lanka, China, Japan, Korea, and much of Southeast Asia, where it is still practiced today.

European Conquerors Arrive

In 327 B.C., the Greek general, Alexander the Great, crossed into northwest India. He conquered a large part of Indian territory, but soon his tired generals persuaded him to return home. One of his generals, Nearchus, commented on the native people: "The dress worn by Indians is made of cotton produced on trees…[they wear] an undergarment of cotton, which reaches below the knee halfway down to the ankles, and an upper garment, which they throw partly over their shoulders and partly twist in folds around the heads…They also wear earrings of ivory…use parasols as a screen from the heat…and wear shoes made of white leather, elaborately trimmed while the soles are of great thickness…".

Contact between the two cultures also left a lasting impact on Indian art—sculptures of the region bear a strong Greek influence.

The Mauryans (321–184 B.C.)

Because Alexander left India quickly, the power vacuum his departure created set the stage for the first great conqueror of Indian history, Chandragupta Maurya (reigned 321–297 B.C.), who created the first unified Indian state.

Chandragupta loved extravagant state occasions, which enabled him to show off his power and wealth with great parades of horse-drawn chariots and elephants decked in gold and silver. He built great palaces, with golden pillars decorated with silver birds. In shady parks planted with imported trees, the royal party would boat on artificial lakes stocked with fish.

This painting shows the god Krishna sitting with his consort, Rahda. They both wear traditional Indian clothes with strands of beads across their torsos. In Indian art, Krishna is usually painted blue.

The state owned huge farms manned by laborers and slaves. Farmers grew rice, wheat, millet, sugarcane, and barley, while others looked after livestock. Cattle provided milk, and they were a source of leather, horn, and hair, used in crafts. Gold and silver were mined, and reservoirs and roads were built.

Chandragupta's son, Bindusara (297–272 B.C.), extended the Mauryan empire over almost the whole of India, but it was Ashoka (286–231 B.C.) who was the greatest Mauryan ruler. A great general in his own right, he was deeply upset by the bloodshed of the battlefield and renounced war to convert to Buddhism. He began to transform Indian society, preaching religious tolerance and vegetarianism and abolishing the death penalty. In addition, Buddhist monks were sent all around Southeast Asia and the Middle East. In 184 B.C., the last of the Mauryan kings was assassinated, and the first empire of India came to an end.

Textile Sophistication

The Mauryans achieved a high level of refinement in textile, clothing, and jewelry techniques. Cotton, silk, wool, linen, and furs were readily available. *Kaseyyaka* (high-quality cotton or silk) was quite valuable.

These three wealthy local landowners are heavily bejeweled with earrings, necklaces, armbands, and bracelets. They are also bare-chested.

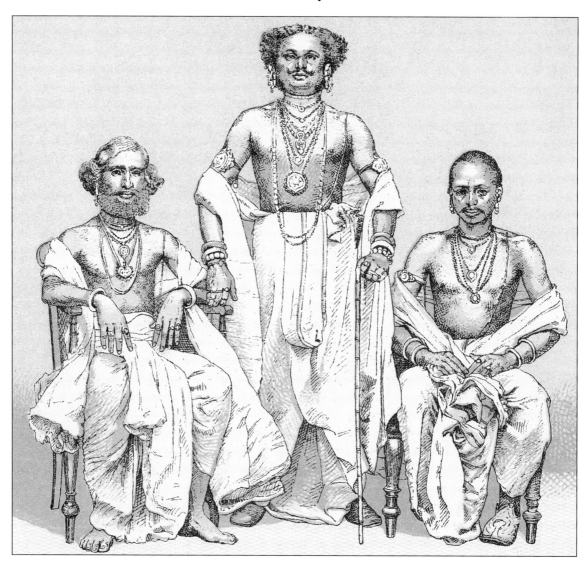

Men and women continued to wear the *antariya, kayabandh* sash, and *uttariya,* as in Vedic times. The *uttariya* was made of white cotton, linen, or **muslin**. The *antariya* was wrapped around the hips and pulled between the legs in the *kachcha* fashion.

The *uttariyas* of upper-class women were decorated with elaborate borders and often worn as a head covering. They also wore fine, transparent muslins embroidered in purple and gold and sometimes precious gems, which were later called *shabnam* ("morning dew"). Also, this is when the *sari* first appeared; archaeologists found one draped around a terra-cotta statue.

The commoners wore simple varieties of the cotton *antariya.* Later in the period, men wore **turbans**, which are still seen today. Their long hair was often twisted into a braid along with the turban cloth. They also often had tattoos. The more primitive forest tribes wore garments made from grass, skin, and fur.

Color was important, and textiles were dyed red (using safflower and madder), white (through bleaching), yellow (the natural color of yarn), and blue (using **indigo** leaves).

Both men and women wore a lot of jewelry. Although the workmanship was initially crude, it later became much more refined, with the use of gold, pearls, coral, rubies, sapphires, glass, and crystals. These were used for earrings (*karnika*), necklaces, armlets, bracelets, and belts. Necklaces often had an amulet in the center for warding off evil spirits.

Religious Robes

As we have seen, religion was extremely important in Indian society, and the priests and monks of the various faiths developed their own dress codes. The wandering Hindu holy men, called *sadhus* (holy women were called *sanyasins*), wore a skirt-like garment that was made of strips of cloth, bark (*valkala*), or leaves sewn together, as well as a short rectangular cloak. The hair and beard were allowed to grow and were braided and arranged in a spiral on the top of the head. This was their appearance for centuries.

Buddhist monks, called *bhikshu*, shaved their heads and beards, but kept the head covered with a headdress. As they had given up all possessions, their clothes were made of rags patched together and dyed with **saffron**. This produced a strong yellow color that still distinguishes Buddhist monks today. In later centuries, monks became rich and powerful and their robes became symmetrical pieces of high-quality cloth stitched together.

Southern Empires: The Satavahana Empire (200 B.C.–A.D. 250)

The Satavahana (or Andhra) empire was established in south and central India around the Deccan, a plateau region between two chains of mountains. Some of the greatest Buddhist architecture, in the form of shrines called *stupas*, was built around this time.

It was a peaceful and prosperous period, and, as with all southern economies, foreign trade was important. The Satavahanas traded extensively with the Romans, who brought in a flow of gold that enriched their empire.

The people of the Deccan were a hybrid race, a mixture of the native Dravidians and foreign settlers. In the first century B.C., their costumes, too, were a mixture of foreign and native garments.

The production of cloth and trade in textiles flourished during the Satavahana period. The region was and still is one of India's richest textile-producing areas. Cotton, silk (for the rich), hemp (for the poor), indigo, and other dye-yielding plants were grown, and many craftsmen were skilled at weaving, **printing**, dyeing, and embroidery.

Embroidery, or "painting with a needle," as the Romans used to refer to it, was an important skill to learn, and it was done exclusively by women. Sometimes, a young lady's suitability as a wife was determined by her ability in this field. Bronze embroidery needles were used from 2300 B.C. in India, but they were probably first used in China in 3000 B.C. Embroidered fabrics, with patterns of flowers, elephants, tigers, swans, peacocks, and the swastika (a

A nobleman prays with a holy man, a *sadhu*, while his boatman waits. The *sadhu* is almost naked. He has uncut hair, beads around his neck, and a rosary in his hands.

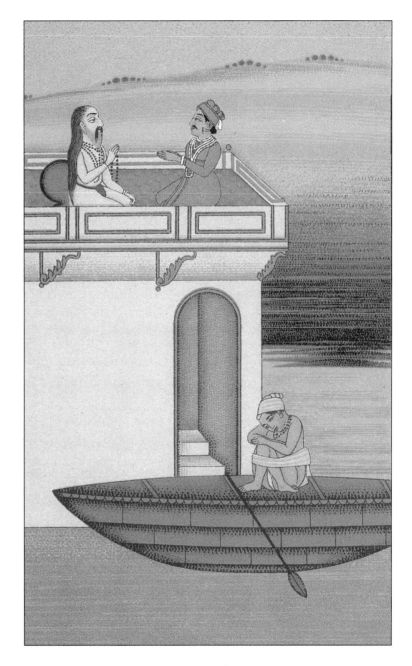

symbol of good fortune), were used to decorate Hindu and Buddhist temples, as well as clothing.

In the Buddhist sculptures of this period, figures appear in stitched clothes. These clothes were different from the ones worn in the north. Stitched clothes—a foreign import—were cut, tailored, and sewn together.

Stiched clothes were worn by members of the king's court, who wore tunics (*kancuka*) and coats. Women, too, wore a short *kancuka,* and, as influences from the north spread to the south, they wore these tunics with short cotton or silk *antariya, kayabandh,* and large *uttariya* with highly decorated borders.

Indian Dancing

Indian dancing has it roots in the Hindu religion, because one of Shiva's roles is as Nataraj, the Lord of the Dance. Dancing was part of temple life, and dancers were known as *devadasis*.

There are four main types of dance: Bharat Natyam, Kathak, Kathakali, and Manipuri. Women perform the first dance, which is quite popular, depicting events in the life of the god Krishna. The dancers always dance with bent knees and never stand upright. Dancers usually wear a *sari* draped to form pleats in the front, which fans out between the legs of the dancers as they move.

Kathak was similar to Bharat Natyam before it became a form of royal entertainment. Intricate foot movements are its hallmark, and dancers usually wear *salwar* trousers and ankle bells that sound as the dancers move their feet.

Men, on the other hand, dance the Kathakali, which tells the stories of dramatic battles between gods and demons from the Hindu holy books, such as the *Ramayana* and the *Mahabharata*. The costumes are equally dramatic. Dancers wear huge, brightly colored skirts and headdresses, elaborate masks, and detailed makeup. The makeup is to emphasize that the characters are superbeings from another world, and different personalities wear different colors. Heroes wear green face paint; evil characters wear a red, black, or white beard; characters representing primitive man wear black makeup; and the gentler, less aggressive characters have yellow or orange face paint. All characters also have their eyes painted red.

Manipuri dances are folk dances. The female dancers wear hooped or stiff skirts with rich embroidery and cone-shaped caps on their heads, all of which are unique to this type of dance.

The figure on the left is a Bharat Natyam dancer. Her earrings, nosering, bracelets, and short top are reminiscent of those worn by Latchimi, the goddess of beauty. The other figures are musicians, dressed in a variety of stitched and nonstitched clothes.

The Kushans of the North

The costume of the Kushan empire of the north (130 B.C.–A.D. 185), which existed at the same time as the Satavahanas farther south, was a product of a thriving textile trade and was a mixture of European, Asian, and Indian styles. The Kushans were the descendants of the Yue-chi tribe of northwestern China, and for the first time, trade with China was directly established through the ancient silk routes.

In addition to the usual *uttariya, antariya,* and *kayabandhan,* they wore stitched clothes, including gowns, tunics, blouses with buttons, skirts, and **paijamas**, quilted coats, Greek **chitons**, **caftans**, and high boots. However, men and women started to leave their heads uncovered during this period, as turbans and veils went out of fashion.

The Golden Age and the First Muslims

When the last of the Mauryan kings was assassinated in 184 B.C., India returned to a collection of separate kingdoms. During this period, the most powerful kingdoms were in the Deccan, a plateau region between two chains of mountains. In the north, however, another major empire was growing, which ushered in one of the most creative periods in Indian history.

The period of the Gupta Dynasty is regarded as a golden age. Chandragupta II (A.D. 376–415) was a great Gupta king. Known as Vikramaditya, meaning "The Sun of Power," he ruled over the greatest cultural age in India. The nobles of the period were great patrons of the arts—including architecture, sculpture, painting, literature, music, and dance—and they attained classical status.

Gupta poetry is full of references to clothes, particularly the sensuous nature of women's clothing, and, indeed, the textile trade remained a major source of

An emperor leads his men into battle on a horse covered in chain mail. Armies also rode into battle on camels and elephants.

income. Fabrics were exported to Southeast Asia and to the eastern Mediterranean areas of Europe and Asia. In the domestic market, too, there were strong links between the north and the south. Textile manufacture developed into a major industry, and silk, muslin, **calico**, linen, wool, and cotton were produced in large quantities. These were printed, painted, dyed, and richly patterned either during weaving or with embroidery.

The art of creating fine, almost transparent muslins was already known, and these had fanciful names. "Evening dew" (muslin that looked like droplets of water), "running water" (muslin that became invisible when dipped in water), and "woven air" (a length of muslin that could pass through a narrow ring) are a few of the names that indicate the fine quality of the fabrics. These names even found their way into Indian poetry and were spoken about as "moonlight on the tulip" or "dewdrop on rose."

Maharajas were princely rulers, and, as can be seen from the number of attendants and huge throne belonging to the traveling maharaja in this image, they were extremely powerful and wealthy.

The History of the *Sari*

The *sari* is now the most common female garment popularly associated with India. Basically a single piece of unstitched cloth made out of silk or cotton, the *sari* is wrapped around a woman's body to form an upper and lower garment.

It was first mentioned in the ancient Indian holy epic, the *Mahabharata,* and was most likely first worn in around 200 B.C. It also appears in the Gupta period, although it is not clear whether these early examples were made of a long single piece of cloth or two pieces joined together.

Exactly when the skirt and veil most women wear were combined into one garment is not clear. One theory suggests that the separate lengths of cloth were too revealing for the Muslim rulers during medieval times, and, therefore, a more substantial body-covering garment was needed.

Another theory suggests that the *dhoti,* worn until the 14th century by both men and women, started to become longer, and the accessory cloth worn over the shoulders was woven together with the *dhoti* into a single cloth to make the *sari.*

The art of printing greatly improved, and many of the fabric designs seen today in India originated in the Gupta period. There were plaids, stripes, and bird and animal patterns, including geese, swans, deer, elephants, and camels.

Royal Dress

Since the time of the Kushans, stitched clothing was linked to royalty, and during the Gupta period, royals appeared on coins wearing coats, trousers, and boots. They also wore the **indigenous** *antariya, uttariya,* and *kayabandh* for everyday occasions. The king's costume was usually blue-striped, closely woven silk with an *uttariya.* The royals imported expensive silk fabric studded with clusters of pearls, called *stavaraka,* which was made in Persia (present-day Iran). These fabrics highlighted the fullness of the body, giving it a relaxed, graceful look. In the Ajanta Caves, carvings depict women wearing full-length *saris.*

Changes in Attitude

During the Gupta period, an increasing number of foreign settlers arrived in India, and this coincided with Indian women clothing the top half of their bodies. The *choli,* an ancient, stitched, square piece of cloth worn on the upper half of the body and originally used by women in Bronze Age Germany, was used for the purpose of modesty. Today, the *choli* is often highly decorated with embroidery and small mirrors that are supposed to reflect evil spirits.

Further outside influences were felt with the introduction of the Persian shirt, or *kurta.* This was popular with both men and women. The popularity of

Hairstyles in the Gupta Period

The Gupta period was one of incredibly elaborate hairstyles—and the rise of expert hairdressers to create them. Huge numbers of flowers, such as the lotus flower, were used to decorate the styles. On top of this, types of hair nets called *ratnajali* or *muktajala*—elaborately jeweled with pearls or gems—were worn.

This passion for hair was so popular that in some parts of India, such as the Deccan, it extended to the lower castes, who usually had neither time nor money for such matters.

Men, too, had their own styles. Their hair was generally worn loose, long, and curled, sometimes with a string of pearls on top. Short hair also became fashionable. However, these bare-headed hairstyles did not find their way into royalty, and high officials still wore the turban.

Shown above are three different styles of Indian turbans, the traditional headdress for men. All Indian men wore turbans, although now it is associated with the Sikh religion in the Punjab in northwest India.

the *uttariya* eventually waned, and it became an accessory instead of an item of clothing. Jewelry for both men and women was exquisite, especially the *vijayantika,* a necklace made from pearls, rubies, emeralds, and diamonds.

Religious dress also changed. The wandering Hindu *sadhus* and *sanyasi* started wearing red **ocher** robes instead of the bark garments, which made them resemble the Buddhist *bhikku,* except that the latter now had their robes made out of linen and silk.

End of an Empire

The Huns, who originally came from China, attacked the Guptas, and by A.D. 480, northern India came under their rule. By A.D. 550, the last of the Gupta kings died, along with their empire. However, as with all invaders, the Huns gradually mixed with the native population and they, too, weakened. Thus, India again broke up into small warring kingdoms.

Despite this, innovations in costume continued to appear. By the seventh century A.D., an increasing variety of stitched garments were worn. The *uttariya* was gradually replaced by tunic-like garments worn over the *paijama* or a *dhoti*. However, this age of cultural flowering eventually came to a radical end as a new and dominant force appeared from Afghanistan, bringing with it a new religion and culture: the Muslim conquerors had arrived.

In the South

From the 6th to the 13th centuries, conflicts between three powers dominated southern India: the Chalukyas, the Pallavas (followed by the Cholas), and the Pandyas. Unlike the growing empires in the north, these kingdoms were small. Despite the constant wars between the kingdoms, empires, and invaders, India kept its Hindu roots, which united the country.

Royal Indian clothes were designed to spread out whenever the wearer sat down on the floor. This gave him or her an air of importance.

Hinduism developed, and the arts flourished. The temple was the focus of Hindu society and the center of textile guilds. Guilds were associations in which craftsmen worked together to produce high-quality fabrics and jewelry.

In these warmer southern regions, royalty still wore unstitched garments, but new names for familiar garments began to appear, showing regional variations. The *uttariya* became the *dupatta, chadar,* or *odhani;* and the *antariya* became the *dhoti.* A Chalukyan king named Someshvara described the use of color and fabric during the different seasons: "smooth, light, and beautiful" garments made of cotton and linen in the spring; "soft and light, smooth and

Islam and the Muslims

Islam, the religion followed by Muslims, was founded in A.D. 570 by Muhammad in Mecca, in what is now Saudi Arabia. In A.D. 610, Muhammad had his first revelation from Allah (God), and this, along with subsequent visions, were written down to form the holy book of the Muslims, the Koran.

Within two decades, most of Arabia had converted to this new religion, which eventually spread to Persia and India, where, although it was the religion of the invading rulers, never made a great impact on the primarily Hindu population.

Islam is associated with a particular type of women's garment called a *burqa.* This is a long, plain outer garment and veil, usually made out of cotton, that covers all parts of the body, from head to toe, except the eyes, and is worn while in public. This garment follows principles laid down in the Koran, which requires women to dress modestly in public. Also, the honor of a Muslim family is said to reside in the conduct of its women. A modest woman, who covers herself up in public and does not show off her looks, commands respect.

billowing" white fabrics in the summer; red, brown, and rose-colored clothes during the rainy season; and saffron-colored wool in the winter.

The First Muslims and the Delhi Sultanate

The emergence of Islam had a dramatic effect on the culture of India. In fact, Arab trading settlements in India were already well established, but it was not until the 12th century that this foothold became permanent. Qutb-ud-din-Aibak established the Delhi Sultanate after assassinating Muhammad of Ghur in 1206. During the Sultanate period, Delhi was the center of Islamic religion and learning. The Sultanate rulers followed the stitched clothing traditions of their homeland, which were woven and embellished with gold embroidery.

Details of clothing are scarce, particularly of women's clothing, because most wealthy Muslim (and often Hindu) women traveled and lived in *purdah*, that is, hidden from the gaze of strangers by a veil while in public, and concealed by a curtain or in a separate part of the house while at home.

A sedan chair was used to carry a rich woman. The covering over the chair kept her from the gaze of strangers, following the *purdah* rules.

This house belongs to a wealthy merchant and is called a *haveli*. It features intricate stone and wood carvings. The best ones can be seen in Rajasthan, in northern India.

Nevertheless, we do know that the Sultanate courts adopted the high-quality Indian fabrics. Muslim royalty set up *karkhanas*, or royal workshops.

The Deccan Sultanates

By the 14th century, the Delhi Sultanate extended southward and established smaller, allied kingdoms of the Deccan. By the 15th century, these kingdoms were strong enough to become sultanates in their own right and became home to Turks, Persians, Arabs, and Africans, as well as Hindus and Muslims.

A distinctive culture resulted from this multiracial society, and the Deccan became a center of learning. Clothes were decorated in rich patterns, and the range of dyes, which did not leak color, made Indian fabrics desirable. In fact, until the 17th century, only India knew the secret of cotton dyeing, and dye-yielding plants, especially indigo, were exported to Europe and the Middle East.

New Invaders: The Moguls and the British

The Moguls, Muslim invaders from Afghanistan, started another golden age in Indian history to rival that of Ashoka and the Guptas. Although there were only six great emperors, whose reigns lasted less than 200 years, the Moguls had a great influence on Indian costume and culture, and started new fashions at court.

Like all previous great dynasties, the Moguls were great patrons of the arts. Painting and literature flourished, but it is the Mogul's passion for extravagant architecture that is best known—they created some of the best-loved buildings in the world.

The first Muhgal (Mogul ruler) was Babur (reigned 1527–1530), who marched from his capital in Kabul, Afghanistan, to Delhi. Babur seems

The Mughal emperor Akbar kept an astonishing 5,000 women in his harem. Three hundred of these were wives, and the remaining women were his mistresses.

unimpressed by what he found in the countryside: "Peasants and people of low standing go about naked. They tie on a thing called *languta,* a decency cloth which hangs two [hand] spans below the belly. From the tie of this decency cloth, another cloth is passed between [the legs] and made fast behind." He is probably describing a short wraparound garment similar to the *dhoti,* which is pulled up high between the legs so that it does not get in the way during work in the fields.

Akbar (reigned 1556–1605), the third great Mogul, came to the throne at only 14 years of age, yet he was able to take full control of his empire. This was

The Taj Mahal

The Taj Mahal is considered one of the most perfect buildings ever created. An incomparable piece of Islamic architecture, the Taj is not a place of worship, but a memorial, built by the fifth great Mogul emperor, Shah Jahan (reigned 1627–1658), for his late beloved wife, Mumtaz Mahal, mother of 14 of his children. Set on the banks of the Yamuna River in Agra, about 125 miles (200 km) south of Delhi, construction of the Taj Mahal began in 1634, and continued for nearly 22 years.

Craftsmen came from all over the known world to work on it. Built entirely out of white marble, it has precious stones set in designs of flowers and calligraphy, all inlaid into the marble. The Taj Mahal changes color during the day, reflecting the pink colors of dawn, the dazzling sun at midday, the orange glow of sunset, and the cool white light of the moon in the evening.

Below the dome, in the dimly lit chamber, lie the remains of Mumtaz Mahal and Shah Jahan, who was later buried beside her, reminding the world of their unending love.

Shah Jahan was fond of big building projects. He also created the Lal Quila, or Red Fort, in Delhi.

largely due to his political skill. He realized that the Hindu population was too large to be controlled by force, so he invited them into his government and army, and allowed them to freely practice their religion.

Aurangzeb was the last of the great Moguls, but he was a fanatical Muslim. Contrary to the rules laid down by Akbar, he attacked the Hindu religion, often tearing down Hindu temples in order to build Muslim mosques in their place. Some of these sites are still disputed by Hindus and Muslims in India today. After his death in 1707, the Mogul empire rapidly fell apart.

Innovations in Court Fashion

The establishment of the Mogul courts brought many innovations in Indian dress. By the 17th century, various elaborate coats appeared: the *jama* (a knee-length stitched frock coat), **choga**, *atamsukh* (an open-fronted robe), and *angarkhas* (another type of long-sleeved gown or coat). These upper garments were worn with equally elaborate *paijamas* and were the height of fashion in the Mogul courts. In fact, paintings and sculptures show that people wore these types of stitched clothes for over 1,000 years in India, although the Moguls did take some of them to new heights. The *choga,* for example, was so elaborate that it could take up to two years to make.

The *jama* was a highly flexible garment and took many forms, depending on the climate and style, in the same way that coats today take many different forms. Often, an undershirt called a *nima* was worn underneath, along with a waistband called a *patka.*

Noblemen and warriors usually carried a dagger called a *katar*. This one has a double gold handle and is for decorative purposes rather than for fighting.

Many foreign travelers were in India at this time. A priest named Chaplain Terry noted the dress:

"The habits both of the men and women are little different, made for the most part of white cotton cloth. For the fashion, they are close, straight to the middle, hanging loose downward below the knee. They wear long breeches underneath, made close to their bodies, that reach to their ankles, ruffling like boots on the small of their legs.

"Their feet are bare in their shoes, which most commonly they wear like slippers. The men's heads are covered with a long thin wreath of cloth, white or colored, which goes many times about them; they call it Sash. They uncover not their heads when they show reverence to their superiors."

The Court of Avadh

In 1590, Emperor Akbar divided Mogul India into 12 provinces, one of which was Avadh. When the empire began to disintegrate after the death of Aurangzeb in 1707, many Mogul nobles left Delhi and headed for Avadh and its capital, Lucknow. The city became famous for luxurious, fashionable, and elegant living. In particular, a ruler named Asaf-ud-Daula began construction of grand palaces and monuments and patronized artists, poets, actors, musicians, jewelers, and craftsmen.

This warrior, holding a sword, is wearing *salwar* trousers, an *achetan* tunic, and a type of *kayabandhan* sash.

In this 18th-century period, a type of *choli* known as the *angia* was fashionable for women and was worn with tunics and vests, similar to those worn by men. Islamic law began to relax for women, and they started to step out of the confines of the *zenana* (the part of the house in which they lived in *purdah*) and participate in the political and social life of India. Various new blouses and jackets followed. The *kanchlis*—simple sleeveless dresses with scoop necks—were worn in parts of Rajasthan and Gujarat, usually with a *ghaghra,* a type of ankle-length drawstring skirt still worn in India today.

With the relaxation of the *purdah,* the forerunner of the modern-day *sari* evolved. Worn with a **petticoat** and a blouse, it was favored by upper-class Hindu and Muslim ladies alike. *Saris* varied in length, ranging from six yards (5.5 m) in the north to nine yards (8.2 m) in the south, and in width from 18 to 60 inches (45–150 cm). All *saris* have a border around the edges. One end, the *palav,* is worn over the shoulder and is often highly decorated.

With unstitched clothes, the difference between the garments of royals and those of the peasants was not in how they were worn, but in the quality of the material. Master craftsmen whose skills were handed down from generation to generation produced the *saris* and *odhanis* in the royal courts. Cities, such as Varanasi, the holiest of Indian cities on the banks of the Ganges, were all centers of excellence for textiles, and the finest *saris* still come from there.

The Arrival of the British

After the Moguls, the next great power was Great Britain, which assumed control following the Battle of Plassey in 1757. The British gradually extended their control over the entire country, but their rule—known as the Raj—was really intended to be a huge money-making project instead of a cultural empire.

Following the example of the Mogul emperor Akbar, the British did not stop the native peoples from practicing their own religions, and they invited many Indian rulers to become part of the administration. These rulers, therefore, retained their status and wealth, although the peasantry suffered greatly. For example, the agricultural policy emphasized commercial crops, such as tea and cotton and indigo dye for the textile industry, instead of essential food-producing crops, and this resulted in numerous famines.

The British undertook many major projects, including starting a smoothly functioning government (moving the capital from Delhi to Calcutta) and building a huge railway and irrigation system that is still used in India today. India became the "jewel in the crown" of the British empire, and slowly Indian society and dress changed to accommodate this new power.

The man on the dais is a Muslim holy man, a *sufi*. He is praying using rosary beads, while his followers pay attention. They are wearing a type of *jama* (long coat) and waistband called a *patka*.

A Mughal emperor rests on his shield. On his hand is a falcon. The jewel on his turban represents the sun, and the feather is a symbol of royalty.

Despite the enormous changes brought by the British and the decline of the Mogul empire, the initial reaction of the Avadh court at Lucknow was to continue as if there had been no changes. *Karkhanas* were set up in the palace complex to provide clothing for the noble families. In addition to the usual *paijamas*, gowns, *odhanis*, *saris*, and *patkas*, the nobles were highly interested in shoes. Various handbags also came into fashion, and, like today, they were designed in a variety of shapes and sizes for holding all types of items, from tobacco to money, jewelry, and toiletries. As this life of luxury became more self-indulgent, women's fashions became highly ornamental. In contrast to previous Muslim eras, clothes became a way of enhancing, instead of concealing, the body.

New Western Influences

As British power grew and became more established, fashions in the courts began to incorporate Western designs. Buttons and collars appeared, and tastes shifted away from the classic unstitched and stitched clothes that had for so long been the staple of Indian dress. Robes became fitted coats, and nobles began to dress in a mixture of native and European styles.

Mass-produced textiles made in European factories began to replace the precious local handcrafted designs, and further changes came from unexpected

The Kashmir Shawl

The shawl has a long history in Asia, but it was in the northern Indian state of Kashmir that the finest ones were made. Originally, the Persian word *shal* (from which we get the English word shawl) just meant high-quality wool fabric and did not refer to any particular article of clothing. Quickly, however, the shawl became a length of fabric draped around the shoulders for warmth. In India, this was essentially a man's garment, and its high-quality wool was usually reserved for the nobility. The Mogul emperor Akbar was fond of them, and such was their prestige that they were often used as bribes instead of money.

Zain-ul-'Abidin (1420–1470) is said to have started the industry, and, from the start, Kashmir shawls were highly prized because of the particular type of **fleece** they were made from. Traditionally, this fleece came from a Central Asian species of mountain goat known as a *pashmina*. The fleece, especially that from the goat's soft underbelly, was collected from shrubs and rocks against which the animals had brushed. However, this was time-consuming, so later, the goats were farmed instead.

A Kashmir shawl was difficult to make. A typical shawl was about five feet (1.5 m) long and two feet (75 cm) wide. One with a complex pattern could take 18 months to complete and involve 12 or more spinners, dyers, pattern designers, weavers, and embroiderers. Women did all the spinning and men did all the weaving, most living in terrible poverty. In Mogul times, the dyes were so sophisticated that over 300 tints were available, mostly extracted from plants and vegetables. Blue came from indigo, orange and yellow came from saffron, red came from logwood, and black came from iron filings.

The borders of the shawl were embroidered and ornamented with bright motifs, such as flowers and birds, using thread of gold, silver, and silk.

sources. For example, the invention of the lightbulb made the metallic thread often used in decorating cloth look too bright, because it now reflected too much light. In addition, all the subtlety created by the reflection of candle flames and gaslight was lost.

Western architecture and furniture styles also influenced the cut of garments. Traditionally, nobles sat on a luxuriously padded floor, strewn with pillows and low stools. Their robes and dresses were designed to spread out on the floor to create a great effect, but as European sofas and chairs became the standard furniture, this became impractical. As a result, clothes styles became slimmer and more fitted.

Women's clothing, however, was not greatly affected by these new Western styles. The *sari* was still the most popular form of dress for women of the nobility right across the country, although even here the traditional handmade garments were replaced with textiles from Europe. Stitched garments went out of fashion, and, to this day, the *sari* is still the single most important piece of women's clothing, whether for Hindu or Muslim.

After the British arrived in India, clothing styles became more mixed. This man is wearing a stitched jacket and loose *paijama*-style trousers, and he is carrying a modern-looking umbrella. He is probably a middle-class trader or businessman.

Ceremonies, Rituals, and Festivals

Special occasions and events marked by ceremonies and festivities occur throughout the year in India. They are an important and colorful part of life, and all communities and faiths have their own. Historically, fabrics and textiles have been associated with these social and ritual events from ancient times.

In the faiths of India, there are various references to aspects of textiles. For example, in ancient Hindu books, the universe is referred to as a woven fabric, and black wool thread is used to ward off evil spirits. Sacred scrolls were always tied in bright pieces of thread, and strips of cloth are still hung on trees and gates around shrines as offerings. Buddha walked on silk when he took his first seven steps, and patchwork cloth is a symbol of unification.

At a Muslim funeral, the mourners wear *kurtas* and *paijamas*. In contrast to Hindus, Muslims are buried with their head facing the holy city of Mecca.

Hair and Religion

Hair is important in many religions. In Hinduism, the birth hair is shaved off after the child's first birthday. Hair is also shaved off when Hindus go on pilgrimage to the holy cities in India. Women let their hair grow for the whole of their married life, then cut it upon the death of their husband.

Sikh men never cut their hair, but tie it in a knot on the top of their head. This uncut hair is called *kesh* and is covered by a turban called a *dastar*. The *dastar* is made from a piece of material about 16 feet (5 m) long and 3 feet (1 m) wide, turned clockwise around the head six times. Sikh women also cover their heads, usually with a long scarf called a *chunni*.

In Muslim dress, proper hair care is a reflection of inner faith and cleanliness. Traditionally, women put oil on their hair and also dyed it with **henna** and *katm*, a plant from Yemen.

Weddings

A huge social and religious occasion, the Indian wedding has its roots in ancient Vedic times. Clothing and ornamentation are highly important. The day before the wedding, the men and women of the bride and groom's families anoint them with a mixture of turmeric (a spice), sandalwood powder, and oil. This herbal paste is used to beautify and cleanse.

The bride is adorned with a lot of jewelry. Bangles called *chaurha* (traditionally made out of ivory) are put on her wrists, and her hands and feet are decorated with designs in henna, a symbol of prosperity and good fortune. A similar ceremony takes place before a Muslim wedding. The bride wears a red and white *sari* called a *bandhani,* named after the **tie-dyeing** technique used to color it. The red color symbolizes fertility and abundance; the white, purity. Her head is covered with the end of her *sari,* and often her hair is full of flowers. The groom usually wears a white *kurta* and *paijamas,* embroidered with golden thread, as well as a head covering, often a turban. Both bride and groom have garlands of roses and marigolds around their necks. In southern India, bride and groom generally leave their heads bare.

Women wear many ornaments indicating their married status. Many of them highlight the regional differences in costume. All married women wear the *bindi* (the dot on the forehead) and the *mangal sutra,* a wedding necklace a wife is traditionally never supposed to take off as long as her husband lives. In southern India, two such necklaces are worn. One is gold, the other a thick thread coated with turmeric. In the west, in Maharashtra, the *mangal sutra* is made out of black beads. In Rajasthan, ivory bangles signify the married state. In Bengal to the east, a white bangle made from a conch shell is worn. Elsewhere, toe rings, bamboo-ring anklets, tattoos, and different ways of wearing a *sari* all show marital status.

Regional Variations

The clothes people wore and how they wore them was one way of telling where they were from. For example, in the desert state of Rajasthan, clothes were brightly colored and embroidered with tiny mirrors to add color to the barren landscape. The traditional dress of women in the region is the *ghagra* (skirt), the *odhani* (head cloth), the *kurti* (a short blouse), and the *kanchi* (a long, loose blouse).

In the northern Himalayan state of Kashmir, the influence of the Muslim invaders can be seen. Men and women wore the *salwar,* a type of trouser also worn in the Punjab, with an upper garment called a

The hookah pipe is used for smoking tobacco by bubbling the smoke through water. It is usually made of brass with a wooden-tipped hose and a brass charcoal-holder at the top.

The Lotus Flower

In India, the lotus flower symbolizes all that is good and beautiful, and the flower appears in Indian folklore and the arts. In Hindu mythology, the lotus flower bloomed with the creation of the universe, and the flower is also a symbol of many other things. Fertility is the most important, but rebirth (since the flower can recycle its own water), purity, and sensuality are all ascribed to it.

Later, Buddhism borrowed the flower from Hinduism. In Buddhist painting and sculpture, Buddha is often shown delivering sermons sitting on a lotus pedestal. For Buddhists, the flower symbolizes independence of the human heart from evil thoughts, because the flower grows in soil, but is itself pure and beautiful.

The lotus flower has many practical uses. The thread, taken from the leaf stalks, is used for making wicks for oil lamps in temples, and an extract from the flower is used in traditional medicine.

pheran (gown) and a skullcap. Since the weather is cold in the mountains, shawls are also popular. In fact, Kashmir shawls were works of art and were highly sought-after by the Mogul emperors.

In the state of Maharastra, the first of the southern states, women's *saris* are made and worn differently from those in the north. It is nine yards (8.2 m) long instead of the usual six yards (5.5 m), as well as slightly wider. This long *sari* is worn all over southern India. Men in the south wear a mixture of traditional Indian dress, the **lungi** or *dhoti,* often worn with a Western shirt. An *angavastram,* a silk or cotton muffler, is sometimes worn around the neck, covering the shoulders.

Today, these differences are not so visible, and men and women wear a variety of clothes from all over India and the Western world. The *sari* is still the

Themes of love were important in Mughal art. Here, a man embraces his lover, while below, a woman greets her suitors.

best-loved women's garment, while men often wear Western shirts and trousers.

Funerals

Funerals are full of ritual. Hindus and Buddhists both believe in reincarnation, in which a person is reborn in a cycle of death and rebirth, before going to heaven. Hindus are cremated, because this is believed to let the soul quickly escape the body. Funerals are conducted by a priest and by the eldest son of the person who has died. A lamp is placed at the head of the body, prayers and hymns are sung, *pindas* (rice balls) are placed in the coffin, holy water is sprinkled on the body, and a *mala* (necklace of wooden beads) or garlands of flowers may be put around the dead person's neck. Women are cremated in a red wedding *sari,* even if they never married—in death, she is considered married to the gods. Widowed women wear white *saris*.

The ashes of the deceased are sprinkled in running water, and the best place to do this is in Varanasi, the holiest of Indian cities on the banks of the Ganges

Trumpeters lead the way at the funeral of a weathly Hindu on his or her way to be cremated. The man behind the musicians carries a pot of holy water to sprinkle on the body.

River. Being scattered into this river ensures that the soul goes straight to heaven, thus ending the cycle of death and rebirth. After the funeral, the widow or widower wears white as a sign of mourning.

Festivals

Indian festivals are colorful and joyous affairs that celebrate events in the religious calendar, as well as particular times of year. The best-known of these is Deepawali or Diwali, the festival of light, which symbolizes the victory of righteousness over evil and the lifting of spiritual darkness. The word *deepawali* literally means rows of clay lamps, which are designed to guide Rama, hero of the Hindu holy epic the *Ramayana,* back home to claim his throne after his exile in the wilderness. The goddess Lakshmi (consort of Vishnu), who is the symbol of wealth and prosperity, is also worshipped on this day.

This festival also marks the beginning of the Hindu new year. Deepawali sees the spring-cleaning and whitewashing of houses, and decorative designs are painted on floors and walls. New clothes are bought, and family members gather together to offer prayers, distribute candy, and light up their homes.

The Sacred Thread

The men of the Hindu Brahmans wear a sacred thread around their torso as a symbol of their closeness to God. This thread is first put on when a boy is between 7 and 16 years old in a ceremony called *upanayanam*. The ceremony is a sign of growing maturity and an induction into the Hindu faith. Three equal lengths of the thread are twisted to form one length.

The boy is also initiated into *Gayathri,* the holiest of all mantras, traditionally chanted by Brahmans. A mantra is a word or piece of text repeated over and over in meditation. The *Gayathri* is a mantra that prays for divine guidance to inspire the mind. It does not seek any personal benefit for the chanter.

In the springtime comes the festival of Holi, a celebration of harvests and fertility of the land. There are many legends concerning the origin of this particular festival. The most popular one among these concerns Prince Prahlad, the god-fearing son of the evil King Hiranyakasipu. Prahlad worshipped the god Vishnu in spite of being persecuted by his father and his demon aunt, Holika. When Prahlad and the gods defeated Holika in a fire, she begged the boy's forgiveness. Prahlad deemed that her name should be remembered on one day each year.

Holi commemorates this event from mythology, and huge bonfires are burned on the eve of Holi as its symbolic representation. During the festivities, people jubilantly cover each other in brightly colored powder and colored water. There are also processions, folk songs, and dances.

There are many other Hindu festival days, as well as the festivals of other religions in India. Muslims celebrate Ramadan, a month of fasting, and the three festivals of Eid. Buddhists celebrate Buddha Purnima or Buddha Jayanti—the birthday of Buddha—in April or May.

The Island of Sri Lanka

The beautiful tropical island of Sri Lanka, formerly known as Ceylon, lies a short distance off the southern tip of India. Although influenced by their bigger neighbor, the Sri Lankans have a unique and distinct culture of their own, with their own history, traditions, and dress.

The country of Sri Lanka, like India, has its own ethnic mix. The majority of the people either regard themselves as Singhalese or Tamil. The Singhalese moved from north India in the sixth century B.C. during Aryan Vedic times, when the legendary Prince Vijaya and 700 compatriots conquered the island.

The Tamils are split into two groups: the Sri Lankan Tamils, who arrived in the 11th century and settled in the north and east of the island, and the Indian Tamils, brought to the island from southern India by the British in the 19th century to work on the tea plantations. Ethnic tensions on the island between the Singhalese and Tamils are still high, with the Tamils fighting to establish their own state in the north of the island.

This photograph of Sri Lankan fruit sellers was taken in 1895. The women and young girls are wearing similar outfits—simple white blouses with cotton *dhoti*-like garments.

Many other foreign groups have also settled here. Arabs known as the Ceylon Moors came in the 12th and 13th centuries, as did Malays. Later, there were Portuguese, Dutch, and British settlers.

Buddhists Arrive

Sri Lanka is best known for its Buddhist traditions, which, as discussed in the first chapter, began in northern India with the enlightenment of Siddhartha

In the early days, Buddhist monks dressed in rags. As their influence grew, they dressed in silk robes, often saffron in color. Note the umbrella, which is a traditional accessory, the fan, and their shaved heads.

Gautama (ca. 563–483 B.C.). During the rule of the Mauryan emperor Ashoka, who in the third century B.C. renounced war to follow Buddhism, missionaries were sent to nine countries, including Sri Lanka. Ashoka's own son, Mahinda, was entrusted with the task of establishing Buddhism in Sri Lanka, which he did with great success.

When Mahinda arrived, the capital of Sri Lanka was Anuradhapura, a city that was presided over by Pandukabhaya (377–307 B.C.). However, most of the population lived in villages. Anuradhapura remained the capital of Sri Lanka for about another 12 centuries. According to Buddhist legend, a sapling was planted there that came from the bo tree under which the Buddha achieved enlightenment in northern India.

Textiles had become an important part of the Sri Lankan economy. Cotton, for example, was grown all over the island as a crop used for trading, as well as for making their own clothes. Sri Lanka also had natural wealth in the form of pearls, precious stones, and ivory from elephants. These resources were not only used in making jewelry for the Sri Lankans—they were also used for trading with foreign merchants.

Small Kingdoms

From the late third century A.D. to the middle of the 12th century, invaders from southern India dominated Sri Lanka. From 1408 to 1438, Chinese forces occupied the island, which had been partitioned into a number of small kingdoms. By the 16th century, the Tamil kingdom was in the north, with the Singhalese kingdoms of Kandy in the center, and Kotte in the south and along the coastline.

In the 16th century, the arrival of the Portuguese in Sri Lanka marked the beginning of European domination, which lasted for more than four centuries. In 1658, the Dutch drove out the Portuguese and took over power; however, in 1796, the British replaced the Dutch. They retained control of the island for more than 150 years.

The skullcaps these children are wearing became popular during the 17th century. Traditionally, a white one indicates a high caste, and red, a lower caste.

Sri Lankan Costume

The *Mahavansa,* the ancient chronicle of Singhalese royalty written in the fifth century A.D., and its sequel, the *Chulavansa,* describe Singhalese dress in ancient and medieval times. The *Mahavansa* states that the Aryan prince Vijaya first spied his wife-to-be, Kuveni, seated under a tree spinning cotton yarn. Legend has it that this took place in the sixth century B.C.; it is said that the ancient inhabitants of the island had considerable cloth-making skills, probably carried out primarily by women.

In ancient times, men went bare-chested, which suited the heat of the low-lying regions of the island. However, kings, nobles, and warriors wore protective clothing and armor.

Unstitched clothes were the most popular form of dress for men for over 2,000 years in Sri Lanka. These would have taken the form of an Indian-style *dhoti,* wrapped around the waist to below the knees. After the Portuguese arrived in the 16th century, European tailored clothing became fashionable and ancient forms of dress started to disappear.

In cooler areas in the hills, people wore a mantle, a cloak-like garment. The kings of the time also wore these, both as fashionable dress and as battle costume. According to the *Chulavansa,* the 12th-century king Parakrama

Bahu I wore a red mantle when traveling up-country. Men, especially those of the higher classes, sometimes also wore robes. Kings, of course, had the best ones, often made out of expensive silk.

However, by the 17th century, garments for the upper body were popular among the male Sri Lankan nobility. The British historian Robert Knox, who traveled in Sri Lanka at this time, wrote:

"The nobles wear **doublets** of white or blue calico, and about their middle, a cloth, a white one next to their skin, and a blue one or of some other color or painted, over the white: a blue or red sash girt about their loins, and a knife with a carved handle wrought or inlaid with silver sticking in their bosom." These doublets were also popular with the lower classes, and both men and women wore them.

Caps were popular as headwear during the 17th century. Higher castes wore either white or blue. Lower castes wore red.

The women of ancient Sri Lanka, like their Indian counterparts, did not cover the upper part of their bodies, but wore a cloth around their hips when at home and another to cover their shoulders whenever they went outdoors. By the fifth century A.D., it was a symbol of status among aristocratic women to be bare-breasted, although heavily bejeweled, while their lower-class female attendants wore a supporting breast band. Upper-class women also wore more elaborate lower garments, such as a *dhoti*-like striped garment.

Robes for women, as for men, were not unknown. A 10th-century inscription refers to a queen

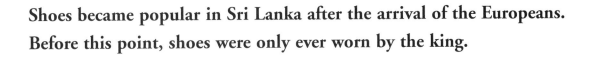

Shoes became popular in Sri Lanka after the arrival of the Europeans. Before this point, shoes were only ever worn by the king.

wearing a blue robe. In fact, women held an honored position in society and enjoyed considerable freedom in political and cultural life. For example, women could own property and inherit royal titles.

By Kandyan times (the 16th to 19th centuries)—in a complete reversal of earlier times—respectable women covered their upper bodies, while women of the lower castes were prohibited from doing so. Also during the Kandyan period, the *osariya* (also known as the Kandyan *sari*) gained popularity. However, it appears that this dress was restricted to women of the Govi caste, the farmer aristocracy similar to the landed gentry in Europe. This caste dominated the affairs of the Kandyan kingdom.

With the coming of the Portuguese in the early 16th century, Singhalese costume underwent a dramatic change. Out went the traditional unstitched clothing, and in came European forms of dress, such as shirts, trousers, blouses, **bodices**, and shoes, which gained wide popularity among common people. The wearing of shoes was particularly interesting, since these, along with stockings, were once worn exclusively by kings.

This Sri Lankan nobleman is wearing a mixture of styles, with a silk Indian-style *dhoti* lower garment under his European-style knee-length buttoned coat, which is topped with a red sash that holds his sword.

Lucky Jewelry

Clothing and jewelry have long held religious and symbolic importance in both India and Sri Lanka, and they are visible in all areas of life. The Sri Lankan bride, for example, wears jewelry of great significance. In addition to a *sari* stitched with gold or silver thread, ornamented with pearls, stones, beads, and sequins, symbols of the sun and moon are placed on either side of her head. These signify eternity in her new relationship with her husband.

Around the bride's neck are several chains, some with pendants (*padakkam*) on them. The swan is an often-used symbol, because it stands for purity and beauty.

Sri Lankans are superstitious about numbers, and odd numbers are considered lucky. Any piece of jewelry, especially a bride's jewelry, is only ornamented with an odd number of stones or gems. In fact, seven is the most magical number, and a bride, therefore, will wear seven pendants around her neck.

Jewelry

The ancient and medieval Singhalese were extremely fond of jewelry. In the *Mahavansa,* Emperor Ashoka in northern India sent presents of lavish jewelry to his Singhalese friend, King Devanampiyatissa. These included necklaces (*pamanga*) and ear ornaments (*vatansa*). Royal women, as in India, wore an array of expensive jewelry, including pearl necklaces (*menik-mala*) worn around the breasts, breastplates (*ora-vasun*), pearl ornaments worn on the arms, anklets (*padagam*), and toe rings (*padanguli*). Women of the lower classes wore rings and bangles that were made of glass. Men, who would have followed the fashions laid down by the king at the time, would also have worn many of these pieces of jewelry.

One important, if strange, piece of jewelry worn by fifth-century upper-class women was the mini-*mevula,* a gem-studded, belt-like covering for the groin. This ornament is often mentioned in classical Sri Lankan poetry and was a symbol of **chastity**, voluntarily worn by women to show off this important status. It differs greatly from the chastity belts worn by noblewomen in Europe, which were forced on them by their jealous husbands while away at war.

In later times, it appears that ornamentation for men declined significantly, and by the 17th century, men wore only rings. Women in Kandyan times,

The Kandy Esala Perahera

Every July and August—a period known as Esala—the hilly Sri Lankan region of Kandy comes alive with a great procession called the Perahera. The Esala Perahera has a long history, dating back to the time the Tooth Relic of the Buddha was brought to Sri Lanka in 304 B.C. This procession lasts 15 nights, and is one of the most colorful and ancient spectacles on the island. Like most Indian and Sri Lankan festivals, its origins are religious, and it is held to honor the Sacred Tooth, one of holiest relics in Buddhism.

The procession, which starts at the Temple of the Tooth Relic, includes drummers, torch and flag carriers, dancers, and about 100 elephants. The elephants are beautifully decorated and wear golden headdresses. A special elephant, the Temple Tusker, carries a gold copy of the tooth relic.

Dancers performing the *uddekki* are accompanied by elephants. Apart from being bare-chested, the dancers wear a white cotton costume. This lower garment, similar to a *dhoti,* stretches down to their ankles. They wear white turbans with the ends left hanging down. They also wear silver earrings and brass armlets, along with beaded straps across their chests, and they carry small hand drums.

With the arrival of the Portuguese in the 16th century, Western fashion became popular. This Sri Lankan woman is wearing a European-style gown and shoes.

however, wore the most extravagant earrings, creating huge holes in their earlobes. Robert Knox, an English sailor in the 17th cetnury, was not impressed:

"Their ears they bore [pierce] when they are young, and roll up coconut leaves and put into the holes to stretch them out, by which means they grow so wide that they stand like round circles on each side of their faces, which they account a great ornament, but in my judgment a great deformity, they being well-featured women." This widening of the ear lobes is no longer practiced.

The Arts

Sri Lankan art, architecture, literature, poetry, music, and dance are all strongly linked to the island's Buddhist traditions. Kandyan dance evolved from village dances performed to appeal to local gods. It used several drummers who banged the *gnh'here*—a wooden drum with monkey skin at one end and cowhide at the other, which made contrasting tones. Dancers often wore devil masks and performed dances symbolizing the defeat of the 18 demons of disease.

Sri Lanka's architecture is also Buddhist-influenced. Massive dome-shaped *dagobas* can be seen all over the country. These shrines are often painted white and contain a holy relic of the Buddha, such as a hair or a tooth. Statues of the Buddha can be found at ancient temple sites, where they are often carved from the rock of cliffs. The Buddha may be standing, reclining, or sitting.

Glossary

Note: Specialized words relating to clothing are explained within the text, but those that appear more than once are listed below for easy reference.

Archaeologist a person who studies material remains (such as fossil relics, artifacts, and monuments) of past human life and activities

Armlet a band (made of cloth or metal) worn around the upper arm

Bodice the upper part of a dress

Caftan a long robe originating in Persia

Calico cotton cloth from Calicut in India

Chastity abstention from all sexual intercourse

Chiton a knee-length Greek robe

Chogas an open-fronted robe, similar to an *atamsukh*

Dhoti a length of fabric worn around the waist to form a lower garment

Doublet a close-fitting garment for the upper part of the body

Embroidery ornamental designs on fabric produced by needlework

Fleece the coat of wool covering a wool-bearing animal (as a sheep)

Henna a red-brown plant-based dye used for decorating the body and coloring hair

Indigenous growing, living, or occurring naturally in a particular region or environment

Indigo a blue dye obtained from the indigo plant

Lungi a length of cloth worn around the waist to form a lower garment, similar to a *dhoti*

Mass-produced produced in a factory instead of handmade

Motif a recurring design or theme

Muslin a fine cotton fabric

Nomadic characteristic of a people who have no permanent residence, but move from place to place, usually seasonally and within a defined territory.

Ocher a red or yellow dye made from mixing clay and iron oxide

Paijamas loose-fitting trousers

Petticoat an underskirt

Printing stamping patterns on fabric

Saffron an orange-yellow dye obtained from a purple crocus flower; also used for coloring and flavoring food

Sari a length of unstitched cloth, six to nine yards (5.5–8.2 m) in length, draped around the top and lower halves of the body to form a garment

Spin to draw out and twist fibers into threads

Stupa a Buddhist shrine, usually having a dome shape

Tie-dyeing a method of dyeing cloth in which patterns are produced by tying up parts of the fabric to resist the dye

Turban headgear worn by men in southern Asia and the eastern Mediterranean area, in which a length of cloth is wrapped around a cap

Timeline

2500–1800 B.C.	Harrapan (Indus Valley) civilization.
1500	Aryans invade; start of the Aryan Rigvedic period.
800	Epic age of Mahabharata and Ramayana.
563	Siddhartha Gautama (Buddha) is born.
540	Vardhamana Mahavira, founder of Jain religion, is born.
327	Alexander the Great of Greece invades northern India.
321	Chandragupta Maurya comes to power and then establishes Mauryan empire.
200	Rise of the Andhra Dynasty in the Deccan plateau region.
130	Kushan empire in northern India begins.
A.D. 185	Kushan empire ends.
250	End of Andhra empire (Satvahana).
320	Chandragupta I establishes the Gupta Dynasty.
376	Chandragupta II comes to power and a golden age begins.
550	End of the Gupta empire.
570	Muhammad, founder of Islam, is born in Mecca.
1206	Qutb-ud-din-Aibak establishes the Delhi Sultanate.
1469	Guru Nanak establishes the Sikh religion.
1634	Death of Shah Jahan's beloved wife Mumtaz Mahal; construction of the Taj Mahal, his monument to her, begins.
1757	Battle of Plassey; the British defeat Siraj-ud-daulah.
1857–1858	The Indian Mutiny; discontent with rule by the East India Company results in sieges and massacres of white people; after the revolt is put down, the country's government is taken over by the British Crown.
1877	Great Britain's Queen Victoria proclaimed Empress of India.
1947	India is granted independence from Great Britain.

Online Sources

Dances of India
www.4to40.com/discoverindia
A detailed look at the Indian culture and costume through the various forms of Indian dance.

India Heritage
www.indiaheritage.org
A site providing short essays on ancient, medieval, and modern aspects of Indian life.

Internet Indian History Sourcebook
www.fordham.edu/halsall/india/indiasbook.html
A superb site with extensive links for exploring the history of India, from 5,000 years ago to the present day.

Sri Lanka Profile
www.lanka.net
An overview of Sri Lanka's geography, history, and modern life.

WWW Virtual Library: Sri Lanka
www.lankalibrary.com/rit.html
An exceptional site providing extensive links to all aspects of Sri Lankan history and culture.

Further Reading

Alkazi, Roshen. *Ancient Indian Costume*. Delhi, India: National Book Trust, 1985.

Askari, Nasreen, and Rosemary Crill. *Colours of the Indus*. London: Merrell Holnerton (V & A Museum), 1997.

Barnard, Nicholas. *Arts and Crafts of India*. London: Conran Octopus, 1993.

Deneck, Margaret-Marie. *Colour Library of Art: Indian Art*. London: Hamlyn, 1967.

Flynn, Dorris. *Costumes of India*. London: Tricolor Books, 1985.

Frater, Judy. *Threads of Identity*. New Jersey: Grantha, 1995.

Garcia, Carol Henderson. *Culture and Customs of India*. Westport, CT: Greenwood Publishing Group, 2002.

Irwin, John. *The Kashmir Shawl*. London: Her Majesty's Stationery Office (V & A Museum), 1974.

Kumar, Ritu. *Costumes and Textiles of Royal India*. London: Chrtisties Books, 1999.

Markovitz, Claude. *A History of Modern India 1480–1950*. London: Anthem Press, 2002.

About the Author

Conor Kilgallon has been an editor for 10 years for a variety of leading publishing houses in London. He has edited a number of successful illustrated books for organizations such as the BBC, The Sunday Times newspaper, and The Discovery Channel. A trained journalist, this is his first book.

Conor would like to thank Gita Kharicha for her help and enthusiasm.

Index